This Journal

Belongs To

_____

Dear God,

I am giving this concern to you.

I know you will resolve this in the

Best possible way for all

concerned.

Amen

Give It To God And Know Peace

Journal

2nd Edition
Hope Winters

Bible Verses from:
The King James Version
The New King James Version

Artwork:
Elena Medvedeva
Tatiana Cheusova
Olayla

"Come to me, all you who are weary and burdened, and I will give you rest."

Matthew 11:28

"The Lord gives strength to his people;
the Lord blesses his people with peace."

Psalms 29:11

Date:

"The Lord will fight for you; you only need to be still."

Exodus 14:14

Date:

"Out of my distress I called on the Lord; The Lord answered me and set me free. The Lord is on my side; I will not fear. What can man do to me."

Psalms 118:5-6

"Cast your burden onto the Lord and he will sustain you; he will never permit the righteous to be moved

Plasms 55;22

Date:

"For I know the plans I have for you, declares the Lord, plans for welfare and not evil, to give you a future and a hope."

Jeremiah 29:11

"Peace I leave with you; my peace I give to you. Not as the world give do I give to you. Let not your hearts be troubled, neither let them be afraid."

John 14:27

Date:

Date:

"Do not be anxious in anything, but in everything by prayer and supplication with thanksgiving let your requests be made known to God. And the peace of God which transcends all understanding, will guard your hearts and minds in Christ Jesus."

Philippians 4:6-7

Date:

"Fear not, for I am with you, be not dismayed, for I am your God, I will strengthen you, I will help you, I will uphold you with mt righteous right hand."

Isaiah 41:10

Date:

Date:

Date:

Date:

"I can do all things through him who strengthens me."

Phillippians 4:13

Date:

"Anxiety in a mans heart weighs him down, but a good word makes him glad."

Proverbs 12:25

Date:

Date:

"For God has not given us a spirit of fear, but of power and of love and of sound mind."

2 Timothy 1:7

Date:

Date:

"She is clothed with Strength and dignity, she can laugh at the days to come."

Proverbs 31:25

"Now may the Lord of peace himself give you peace at all times and in every way. The Lord be with all of you."

2 Thessalonians 3:16

Date:

"I will both lie down in peace, and sleep;

For You alone, O Lord, make me

dwell in safety."

Psalm 4:8

"Be strong and of good courage, do not fear nor be afraid of them; for the Lord your God, He is the One who goes with you. He will not leave or forsake you."

Deuteronomy 31:6

Date:

"God is within her, she will not fall; God will help her at break of day."

Psalms 46:5

Date:

Date:

"My grace is all you need, for my power is the greatest when you are weak."

2 Corinthians 12:19

Date:

"Do not grieve, for the joy of the Lord

is your strength."

Nehemiah 8:10

Date:

"It is God who arms me with strength,

and makes my way perfect."

Psalms 18:32

Date:

"And we know that in all things God works for the good of those who love Him, who have been called according to his purpose."

Romans 8:28

Date:

"But I will sing of your strength, in the morning I will sing of your love; for you are my fortress, my refuge in times of trouble."

Psalms 59:16

Date:

Date:

"To everything there is a season, a time for every purpose under heaven."

Ecclesiastes 3:1

Date:

"I have heard your prayers, I have seen your tears; surely I will heal you."

2Kings20:5

"The Lord your God in your midst, The Mighty One, will save; He will rejoice over you with gladness, He will quiet you with His love, He will rejoice over you with singing."

Zephaniah 3:17

Date:

"Trust in the Lord with all your heart,

and lean not on your own

understanding."

Proverbs 3:5

Date: